TULLMAN ON
COMPANY CULTURE

TULLMAN ON
COMPANY CULTURE

HOWARD TULLMAN

BLOG
into**BOOK**

Blog Into Book
www.BlogIntoBook.com
Cover portrait by Matthew Cherry
Drawing by James "Red" Schmitt
Edited by Jasmine Slivka
Copyright © 2014 Howard A. Tullman
All rights reserved.
Other books by Howard Tullman:
The Perspiration Principles

CONTENTS

TELL A SIMPLE STORY

Almost every day I meet and speak with young entrepreneurs trying to get their new businesses off the ground. I don't generally have a lot of time, but I always try to give anyone at least a few minutes to explain what they're trying to do and then I can decide very quickly whether it makes more sense to meet further with them. Frankly, what you can't basically say in ten minutes about your business or your idea really isn't worth saying. I don't think of these little chats as "pitches" (elevator or otherwise) – they're much more like speed dates where you're trying to decide very quickly whether what you're hearing makes sense; whether there's a real business or opportunity lurking there; and whether the person you're speaking to has the passion, enthusiasm and smarts to turn a good idea into a real business.

After 50 years of doing this, I can tell you that it's actually possible to make these initial decisions with a high degree of accuracy in a matter of minutes. Now I admit that I will definitely miss out on a few real opportunities and turn down or not pursue some very talented people, but, by and large – especially since we're all dealing with limited time and scarce resources – the system works and works pretty well.

And here's the main reason why – it's not that I'm so perceptive and smart; it's that way too many people make it too easy to turn them down because they're so unprepared to take their best shot in the moment when the opportunity is there and because they don't really understand how to make the most of that short window of time.

As we used to say in the music industry, it's really easy to tell when a song is bad, but only the public and the market will ultimately decide what sells. Note that I said "what sells", not necessarily what's good. The music business today is all about selling disks and downloads, not making great music. Always has been; always will be.

And it's the same story with describing new businesses. If you're all over the place; if you're trying to be all things to too many people; if your story is so complicated that it's hard to even follow; or if you've got a solution in search of a problem, it's going to be pretty easy to say "thanks, but no thanks". You've got one shot, one moment, and one opportunity to get right to the heart of the matter and the most crucial part of the entire process is to tell a simple story.

How simple? Your story should answer 3 simple questions about your company which, by the way, are the very same questions that will inform and guide your company for its entire existence. These answers are also every bit as significant for each and every employee as they are for any investors. So it's pretty important to get the answers right at the outset. The answers might change over time, but the fundamental questions never do.

Here they are:
Who are We?

Management and team members' relevant experience and credentials

Where are We Going?
Short and long term objectives and goals – abbreviated milestones – timeframe

Why?
What problem is being addressed and solved – time, money, productivity, status

Short, sweet and to the point. You've got to be a ruthless editor and there's no question that the hardest choices are about what to leave out, not what to include. You need to think of both detail and elaboration as forms of pollution. Cut to the quick. And stick to your story.

One of the nastiest things venture guys like to do to "newbies" is to ask them how big their businesses can be and how many opportunities and directions there are to grow the businesses. And when they charge off into the future and start building their castles in the sky; the VCs look at each other, roll their eyes, and say to themselves: "Boy, this guy's not focused at all."

It's an old but important trick from debate class – tell the story you need to tell, be relentless, stay on point, keep it short, and make the limited time that you have count. Everything else can come later. Bottom line: tell a simple story.

YOU CAN'T ADD VALUE IF YOU DON'T HAVE VALUES

For new businesses, there are lots of things you just can't afford financially. Those things are typically (and painfully) pretty obvious. And I'm not just talking about fancy cars, frills, and bells and whistles. I'm talking about fairly basic, but sadly expensive, stuff. The good news, however, is that, as you grow your business, a lot of these kinds of problems will go away. I like to say that any problem that you can solve with a check isn't really a problem at all – it's just one of a million different choices you'll have to make as time goes on.

But there are a bunch of other things that start-ups also can't afford that have nothing to do with money. One of the most complicated and least talked about (in this feel-good, politically correct world we live in) is real values. You absolutely cannot afford to have the wrong values when you're building your business. In a word, you can't be pushing platitudes when you're trying to make payroll.

It makes me sick to read these retrospective (rewrite my life please) articles by people who've made it (sometimes thru hard work; sometimes thru luck; sometimes thru family ties or special connections; and sometimes for no apparent reason at all) talking about how important it was to their success that they had all these Mom & Pop, Apple Pie, and democratic (small "d") values as part of their businesses from the beginning. It's a complete crock. And what's worse is the fact that it can mislead other people into thinking that this is the way the real world works. But it's not.

As sad as it may sound and as bitter a pill as it may be to all the bleeding hearts and social scientists out there that have never run anything, the truth is that you need to adopt the values that are right for your business from time to time. As the joke goes, "These are my principles. If you don't like them, I have others.", but it's not really a joke. As a new company, you can't afford the luxury of having grown-up, fancy values when you are fighting for survival. And anyone who tells you otherwise just hasn't ever been there in the trenches looking right into the bottom or the wrong end of the barrel.

Now I'm not saying, of course, that you shouldn't have any concrete values, I'm just saying that the values that will make or break your business should and will change over time as your business and your team matures. This is actually a lot easier to show you than to try to describe. But first let me give you a few basics:

(1) Your core values need to be manageable and realistic for your business.

(2) Your core values need to be relevant to your business and your employees – not generic, but unique.

(3) Your core values need to be short and memorable – the

shorter the better – ideally they'd all fit on the back of your business card.

(4) Your core values need to be as simple as possible, but no simpler.

(5) Your core values need to be repeated constantly and internalized by everyone in the company.

At TFA, my college, our five core values are clear to all. We believe in:

>Unstinting Effort
>
>Pride of Craft
>
>Courage of Our Convictions
>
>Loyalty
>
>Excellence

Now, here are five core values from a large, mature corporation in our marketplace:

>Fairness
>
>Respect
>
>Opportunity
>
>Security
>
>Inclusion

I hope the differences are obvious. Not one of these words conveys any energy or a bias for action. They're pretty much entirely devoid of emotional content. And even if I knew what some of these words were intended to mean in the way of behavioral guidance, they don't tell me jack about what makes the company stand up and stand out every day. If you still don't get it, here's a visual aid:

Frankly, I couldn't build a fire under any group of employees with a stem-winder about inclusion or security if my life depended on it. In fact, in a start-up, attempts at too much inclusion are like ingesting a slow-acting poison that kills your response times, wastes enormous amounts of time and other resources, and almost always leads to mediocre results. I've said it before and I'll say it again – not every idea is a good idea – not every suggestion is worthy of extensive discussion - and democracy in meetings isn't really a virtue in and of itself. If I had the choice, I'd rather work for a tyrant any day than for a committee.

Again, there's nothing terribly wrong with these kinds of broad, vague values, they're just terribly wrong for a new, young business to try to live by or to live up to. And that's the real crux of the matter. You've got to make your core values real and you've got to make them matter or you're just wasting your breath. Company values don't break, they crumble slowly over time unless they are actively pursued and nurtured. It's a slippery slope and only you can stop the constant threat of erosion.

So, assuming you've got the right ones for your company's developmental stage and size, how do you protect and promote them? Three basic rules:

(1) Make your company values aggressive and demanding

(2) Make them inflexible and uncompromising

(3) Be totally intolerant of breaches

Once your values start to slide, it's almost impossible to recover. And believe me nothing is more central to your company's culture and your ultimate shot at success than getting this process right. You're the values cop.

And nothing is harder because it's NEVER easy to say what no one wants to hear and it's the easiest thing in the world to give someone a temporary pass or to overlook something in the moment when you should jump on it. But remember two important things: (a) past sins never vanish, they just wait; and (b) you can't talk yourself out of problems that you behave yourself into. You've got to insist on the proper behaviors and the proper attitudes and stick to your guns.

It's your job – it's not fun; it's not easy – if it was, we'd all be making $12,500 a year – and it's a constant process that requires continual vigilance.

To make your core values stick, you've got to be prepared to take it to people every day and insist that they get on the program or go somewhere else. Don't confuse someone's good manners with their willingness to change their behavior – you need to make sure that their commitments aren't just words - and that their apologies aren't just lip service. Any apology not accompanied by a change in behavior is an insult.

MAKE ROOM
FOR PEOPLE – PART 1

As your company grows, the most important and hardest decisions that you will make will be about the people you hire and those you have to fire. There's a lot of talk these days about technology, but some things never change and the fact of the matter is that the ONE sustainable competitive advantage that any business can have for the long run is talented, committed and passionate people. Everything else erodes over time – especially technology which eventually in every case becomes accessible, cheaper and more broadly applicable by your competitors

Many years ago I made this chart to track the price-novelty curve of technology which shows how the price of new technology diminishes over time and the other marketplace changes that accompany this process. (You'll get some idea of how old this chart is by noting that the software I used couldn't really even replicate a smooth curve.)

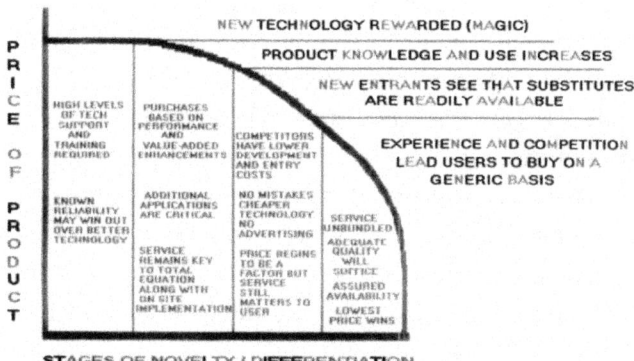

As you can see from the chart, while at the outset, new technology is almost indistinguishable from magic, by the time it becomes widely available and accepted, people basically take it for granted and price drives the discussion. As you can imagine, discussions about the lowest available price are never what we would call "happy talk".

But, good people, well-educated and motivated, just get better, stronger and more valuable all the time – especially if you watch their backs and stay out of their way. The real trick is to find 'em, hire 'em and keep 'em. Equally important is to move quickly to fire the people who aren't making it. Simple rule: Hire slow; fire fast.

(I'll deal with keeping your top performers and firing people who aren't in the next couple of posts, but suffice it to say that virtually NO ONE was ever fired too soon. Once you know that things aren't working out, you almost can't move too quickly to fix the situation. Every day you wait is one day too many and much too late.)

Let me start with a piece of bad news that comes from my friend Jay Goltz who says that CEOs are among the worst possible people to do their company's hiring. Why? Because, by and large, they're (a) short on time and often distracted; (b) great talkers and bad listeners because they're always selling themselves and their businesses rather than asking and learning about the interviewee; and (c) too good-natured and trusting about people and not skeptical enough to ask the hard questions. So you may not be the best person in your organization to do this job even though there are few that are more important.

So consider yourself warned. Now, what can you do to at least give yourself a fighting chance of doing a good job? Here are a few ideas and rules that have helped me over the years:

(1) <u>People lie about their resumes all the time</u>. I'm not saying this to get you down on mankind in general or anything like that. I'm just suggesting that it's perfectly reasonable to ask detailed questions about a resume and to take everything on it with a grain of salt or a tablespoon. I looked younger than my age for years (not sure when things caught up) and I once flew to France for a huge meeting with some folks over there involving millions of dollars. I got there – walked into the room – and was treated so shabbily by these folks (even taking into account that they were French assholes) that I was dumbfounded. I had lunch and went right back to the airport and returned home. I later learned that they saw me and having read my pretty extensive resume decided that I wasn't old enough to have done half the stuff written there and so I must have been lying to them. I wasn't, but it was a real lesson in managing information and expectations that I've never forgotten.

(2) <u>Credentials are not the same as accomplishments</u>. Degrees are nice to have, but it's your deeds and the things you've actually gotten done that matter in the final analysis. And, there are plenty of "smart" people out there who aren't people smart. If you can't get along with the "natives" as part of an effective and collaborative team, your native intelligence doesn't mean squat.

(3) <u>The best person you interview may not be the best person for the job in question</u>. Too many CEOs think that they should hire any great person who comes along and figure out a good job for them later. As important as it is to have super-talented people, trying to "warehouse" them (even when you're growing like crazy) is a losing strategy. Get a clear job description, understand the criteria for a successful candidate, and focus on filling that job.

(4) <u>There are no easy jobs today</u>. Every candidate should have the basic required skills as a starting point. But the right prospects are the ones who have the <u>ability</u> to get the job done. Ability in any area is the successful combination of toughness (mental and physical), resourcefulness (flexibility and adaptability) and powerful concentration (focus and direction).

(5) <u>Gray hair is a sign of age, not necessarily wisdom or relevant experience</u>.

Young and (first-time) CEOs tend to get a point in the early growth of their businesses where they believe that they need to add some "grown-ups" to the management mix. There are usually a number of pretty standard excuses, explanations and reasons offered for these kinds of feelings, but ultimately the real driver is fear: (a) fear of being alone and responsible; (b) fear of being in way over your head; and (c) fear of fucking things up. I can't make the fears go away, but I can tell you that 90 times out of 100 these types of lateral hires fail miserably and you will be the most miserable of all concerned because you did it to yourself and your company. There's not a simple or single explanation for the overwhelming failure rate, but generally the 4 main misses are: (1) a quickly-emergent lack of energy (stamina) and enthusiasm; (2) a totally absent connection to and comfort with the rest of the employees; (3) an early tendency to criticize the way you run the business; and (4) a focus and excessive interest in and emphasis on financial and compensation

MAKE ROOM
FOR PEOPLE – PART 2

Once you've hired some terrific people, the next job is to hang on to them. Interestingly enough, that's getting harder, not easier, to do even in these tough economic times because (a) no one assumes any longer that they'll spend most of their career at the same place and (b) people these days don't commit to companies, they commit to other people and other people change and move on all the time. So how can you keep the stars (and the rest of the troops) happy, healthy and motivated?

First, nothing is more important than making room for people. All kinds of people – because talent comes in lots of different sizes, shapes and packages. We want the talent, but we aren't always willing to understand that it's a package deal. Some people like to work all night; some don't especially care to bath; some are insufferable and brilliant at the same time. You need to make room for these people and run interference for them if you want to build a great company. Too often, entrepreneurs try to find and hire people that look, act and talk like them and this never works beyond the first few employees. You need all kinds of people – even people just looking for a job – not a career and not looking to join your sacred crusade – just as long as they're willing to do their job and do it as well as they can. And honestly, your employees also don't have to love each other or go bowling every Thursday night. They just all need to show up and each do their jobs. Everything else is Kumbaya and gravy.

Second, you've got to talk straight to everyone, tell the truth, and do a couple of administrative things right away: (1) define and nail down each new person's job and the reporting hierarchy; (2) explain your expectations – tell people what you're trying to accomplish and what you're willing to sacrifice to accomplish it and make sure that they're signed up for the same trip; and (3) establish the criteria to measure and evaluate success and confirm in writing that they are understood by everyone.

It's funny, but over the years, you learn that that the people from whom you really learned the real things of value (good or bad) were not the warm and fuzzy folks. They were sharp, hard-edged, driven people with a clear sense of purpose who were always asking more of you. And the real reason that those times were so instructive was that, in the midst of all of the blood, sweat and tears, and occasional screaming, you never doubted for a moment that they believed in you and believed that you were up to the task and could do whatever it took to get it done AND you knew that they would be there working and standing right beside you when you did.

It's great to shoot for the sky and have high expectations and to ask your people to work insane hours and move mountains as long as you never ask them to do anything that you wouldn't do yourself and as long as you're working side-by-side just as hard as they are. This whole area is a slippery slope. Keep in mind that getting the most work out of people isn't necessarily getting their best work. Ultimately, it's a quality, not simply a quantity game. Lots of people learn how to keep busy – the trick is to get things done and done right. Not all movement is progress.

Third, forget all this bullshit that every idea is a good one. Plenty of ideas just suck. Pretending that every idea is possible or worthy of consideration and discussion and trying to be politically correct and always constructive in your criticism is a formula for failure. It's nice to be liked; it's more important to be respected. And sympathy is a lot like junk food – it doesn't help anybody to lie to people or give them false encouragement or hope. Hurt feelings, bruised egos, skinned knees are all part of the growth process and critical to it.

Finally, your people are very important, but don't lose sight of the main chance. The name of the game is to create great products and services and to build a company that will last – it's really not about making people feel good about themselves and loved. Leave that to the clergy. Seeking consensus is about finding the middle ground, settling, and making people feel good about themselves and each other – it's a completely different objective than building your business and it has no place in the rough and tumble world of getting a new company off the ground. You can have higher aspirations, broader goals, and apple pie mission statements once you can pay the bills and afford those luxuries.

In much the same way, teamwork is certainly a wonderful thing, but in a start-up, it's mainly a means to getting the help you need to see your vision through to completion. Political correctness, consensus building and hyper-collaborative teamwork will only take you so far. You can't serve too many masters or chase too many rabbits at the same time or you'll end up with none. You're not a social welfare agency; you're not a church or a charity; and you're not your employees' shrink or family – you're a small, young business trying to grow into something important and that alone is a full-time job and then some.

The truth is that most of the world's great products and businesses – as well as most of the great inventions throughout history – were ultimately the result and expression of a single, uncompromising vision - albeit managed, massaged, and manipulated through a sea of change, confusion and compromise. That's your main job – define, defend and drive the vision. The reason that it's so important to always keep the vision front and center and so inextricably tied to your people is that great ideas can bring people, but ultimately it's something bigger – ideals – that keeps them together. We all want to be working for something that's bigger than ourselves.

In building your business, you have a small window and often a single chance, a passing moment and a fleeting opportunity to make something special and spectacular and to make a difference – if you have the courage of your convictions, the confidence in your abilities, and if you're willing to make and stick to the hard choices that will inevitably arise. The people choices are always the hardest.

MAKE ROOM
FOR PEOPLE – PART 3

There's no more challenging job in a young company than being the person who has to let people go. Everyone else gets to talk about what a tight-knit, stick together group the company is (just like a "family" of friends) and all that other touchy-feely stuff, but you're the one who has to deliver the bad news over and over again. And it's true whether you're the CEO or the head of sales or the HR manager – it doesn't really matter – it's a tough job for anyone. If you were unpopular in high school, you're already one step ahead of the game. It's not easy or always popular to be the boss, but then good leadership isn't a popularity contest. It's a given that you can't please any of the people all the time.

The truth is that your company's only as good as your worst employee and the best-run businesses are always looking to either retrain and upgrade or replace the lowest performing employees. Sometimes it's a breeze. We try to immediately fire any employee who doesn't try or doesn't care. These are cardinal sins in a start-up and there's no question that these people need to go – they're always the easiest decisions. And then the job gets harder and harder.

The next tier of troublesome employees is those who try hard, but just cannot do the job. You can be totally sincere and have the best of intentions, but still be incapable (or no longer capable) of doing the job that needs to get done. There are good people who are perfectly able to do a job poorly for a very long time before anyone has the time, interest, or guts to ask the hard questions about results rather than effort. These people need to go too, but you need to be as fair and firm with them as you can. And do them a real favor – tell them the truth.

Then there are the employees who are basically hard-working and dedicated, but who (for better or worse) can't fit into or model the corporate culture and behaviors. Every business that I've been involved with has ultimately been about hard work mixed in with a healthy dose of paranoia. We had lots of ways to reflect this ethic and plenty of signs all over the place. "Hard work conquers everything." "Effort can trump ability." "We may not outsmart them, but we'll outwork them every time." "Obstacles are those frightful little things you see when you take your eyes off the goal." "Just because you're paranoid doesn't mean that someone's not out to get you." And so on and so forth. And almost everyone we hired got the message and drank the Kool-Aid. Even the people who just wanted a "job" and not a career or to join a sacred crusade pretty much still worked their butts off.

But every so often, we'd hire someone who was just too healthy and well-adjusted to succeed among our tribe of crazies. We used to say that a relaxed man is not necessarily a better man. In one business, our internal motto was "let our sickness work for you". It turned out that it was important to let the other people see you sweat – not just the big deals – but the smallest details so they knew you cared. If you weren't just a little bit crazy about the work and the business, you were slightly suspect or worse.

I remember one special case where after we let someone go he wrote me a long letter and asked for a more complete explanation of why he didn't succeed with us. I decided to reply and ultimately what I ended up telling him is something that it's worth always keeping in mind when you sign up to be an entrepreneur. I wrote:

> *I'm sorry that complex issues like an individual's performance and work attitude get reduced to unfortunate shorthand phrases like "not hungry enough", "didn't want it", etc. in conversations with others who want to know "what happened?". We all know that work and relationships are far more complicated than a few pithy phrases. And we also know that, in their own mind, almost everyone wants to do a good job that they and others can be proud of. But here's the rub. Only a select few individuals are crazy enough (as we pretty much all are here) to subject themselves to the constant stress and heartache associated with starting and building new businesses. Our company is a very fast track run by a bunch of workaholic perfectionists. We all believe that that's what it takes to win against pretty fierce odds. And this is simply not the right place for everyone – especially people who want to have a family, outside interests and a normal life. I think it's very likely that you're simply too nice and too well-adjusted to work with the crazies around here and that's shame on us – not you. But it's the way things are. We wish you all the best.*

Ultimately, all of these situations come down to the basic choice – you can make one person miserable for a period of time when they lose their job, or you can end up with a crappy company where everyone's miserable because you don't have the guts to do the right things for the business. And once you start to carry people along who aren't performing, you take a tremendous <u>double hit</u> – you pay the price for the poor performer's activities, but that's nothing compared to the real harm. As soon as you fail to consistently fire non-performers, you start to lose your best people and that's what kills the company.

To do this right, you have to build a differentiated system from the start that provides different levels of rewards, acknowledgments and compensation for different people throughout the business. And you need to move quickly and regularly to identify and remove the bad apples before they spoil the whole place.

THE ONE WHO CARES
THE MOST WINS

Remember when parents used to really care about their kids talking back to them or cursing? For a time, long after the weight and the sting went out of certain "swear" words and they were just words again in common use – albeit not universally, some kids (mostly younger brothers and sisters) still tried using them for effect and to rile up their folks, but it was pretty clear that no one actually cared that much. Sticks and stones, etc. Plus, and maybe most importantly, saying this kind of stuff and meaning it – even assuming that the kids knew what the words actually meant – were two dramatically different things. And their parents got that, refused to take the bait, and generally let a lot of "noise" just slide.

But their older brothers and sisters didn't waste any time in figuring out the most telling and effective new parental taunts to get under their folks' skins again and they deployed them so efficiently that even the grown-ups got with the program and adopted the new jargon almost overnight. And, somewhat amazingly, it was a single word that said it all for at least an entire generation.

And what was that word? It was **"whatever"** (shoulder shrug optional). In so many ways and so many circumstances and situations, "**whatever**" said it all and got the job done – smoothly and succinctly. And, what exactly does "**whatever**" really mean? It means "I don't care enough to care". So there!

It's one of those things that Aaron Sorkin only wishes that he could have added to the vernacular. For the moment, he'll have to settle for "ya think?" and a few other choice phrases that you can view <u>ad</u> <u>nausem</u> on the various YouTube *West Wing* or Sorkin compilations. And who's the very living embodiment of "**whatever**" every week on our TV screens? Of course, it's Dana Brody, the daughter from *Homeland*. If Carrie cares way too much about everything, Dana pretty much lets her Mom know every single episode that she doesn't much give a rat's ass about anything that her Mom cares about and she sure lets it show.

But why should any of this matter to you? We're pretty much in business after all – not entertainment, TV or the movies. But, as I've said before, no one sells a product any more – we're all in the service business now – where the key deliverable is the ability to create in the customer's mind the feeling of being sincerely cared for and cared about. Frankly, no one cares how much you know or how good you are at your job (except maybe if you're surgeons who apparently aren't required to have a personalities) - until they know how much you care <u>about them</u>. Caring costs a lot, but in the end, your people not caring is what kills businesses.

So the reason that the "**whatever**" phenomena should matter to you and your business is because the real message of "**whatever**" – which is an in-your-face, calculated, and painfully obvious indifference (however sincere or insincere it may be) - is a fact of life these days in too many places and, if you let it creep into your business and particularly into the attitudes of your people, you're screwed. Your customers will leave in droves. And they won't be back.

This is more critical than you think and something that gets overlooked too easily in the frenzy of rapid growth. I'm not talking about warm and fuzzy stuff – or Kumbaya crap – I'm talking about everyday execution of the fundamentals in your business. The truth is that, if as you grow, your people can easily get a little "tired" and think they have too much to do and that customers are a bother and too demanding and somewhat inconvenient, and when they start communicating that indifference to your customers, it's actually worse than you can imagine. It's like a slap in the face to the customers and they will pick up on it in a flash.

Why does it happen? First, it's not necessarily intentional and evil in many cases. Almost anything can get routine and repetitive and it's a short step from there to indifference. Second, passion isn't an infinite resource and it needs to be reinforced and replenished regularly. Third, today's younger employees are hard sells in a lot of ways. You need to keep in mind that at work they are generally more afraid of boredom than failure. And finally, anything that keeps growing and getting bigger always runs the risk of distancing your best people from the immediacy of the constant contact with your customers which is the very best feedback and reinforcement loop there is. Hearing the news – good and bad – from the horse's mouth is critical to keeping your people's heads in the game.

So, just like it's unsafe at night to speed so fast that you "overdrive your headlights" and can't see far enough ahead to safely stop in an emergency, a young company can outrun and outgrow its own energy and enthusiasm as it expands and burn out - not only lots of its loyal customers, but plenty of its best long-time employees as well. And when you do that, you find out that you've ended up with the <u>wrong</u> answer to the universal question: how big can we get before we get bad?

What can you do? You've got to spend the time and the resources to constantly reinforce the main message: that businesses exist because they have customers and taking care of your customers is ALWAYS Job Number One. Everything else can and should take a back seat to making sure that your customers know that you are looking out for them. And you've got to do it with a vengeance – with all your heart and all your energy. You don't get to fake it until you make it in today's super-savvy world. Second, the very best cure for employee boredom and indifference is challenge and curiosity. There is no cure for curiosity and your job is to make sure that your employees are always looking at new opportunities and new challenges. Finally, as always, focus. The smartest people I know care passionately about the few things in their life and in their business that really matter – the right things - and don't waste a minute or give a damn about the rest.

As you're trying to build your business and change the world, it's a good idea to remember that a different world can't be built by indifferent people.

BRICKS AND MORTAR DON'T MAKE A BUSINESS

I see way too many young entrepreneurs spending way too much time and energy worrying about their furniture, fixtures and equipment (FF&E in the trade) way too early in the growth and development of their fledgling businesses. This isn't the way to grow anything that lasts. I like to say: "Let's rob the train before we spend our time splitting up the loot."

In the same way that your company needs to have a changing set of core values as you grow, you need to focus on things at the outset that are a lot more significant than color schemes and coffee tables. There's a right time for everything and – while it's true that people need a decent place to come to work – it's a lot more important to give them some very good and compelling reasons to come to work than to worry about what the place looks like when they get there. Offices are a necessary part of the deal, but they're not sufficient to get the business built if you aren't far more focused on your people and your culture. It's the messaging, not the materials that matter.

Alignment ultimately trumps architecture and design. The reason the *Aeron* chair is so well-known from the dot.com days and such a cliché today isn't because it was a beautiful and well-built chair; it's because these $1200-plus chairs were the complete embodiment of the wretched excess and stupid spending that characterized the self-absorption and arrogance of that time. Build your palace after you're profitable.

In the meantime, there are some things to keep in mind when you are trying to figure out how to have the environment you're putting together support and reinforce the culture and the values that you want to embed in your business from the beginning. This isn't easy to do with scarce resources and limited time, but it's possible if you do what you can and don't overdo it. And please, if you remember just one thing above all, don't try to do something cheaply that you shouldn't do at all. If your budget is brutal, do a few things well and forget the rest. In the long run, quality and smart choices matter most.

In the last ten years or so, with my design partner, Barbara Pollack, we've built out over 300,000 square feet of space for various businesses; made as many mistakes as you can make in the process; and learned a lot about what not to do as well. Here are a few of the most important take-aways.

1. The Ten Second Test – First Impressions Matter

It's a *Head & Shoulders* world – we rarely get a chance to make a second impression so you need to make sure that the first impression people have of your business is at least favorable - and ideally - fabulous. At Flashpoint, the elevators you ride to get up to our main space are tired, slow and tiny. I always tell guests (as we're riding up) that they shouldn't be concerned because the 70 year-old elevators are the oldest technology they're going to see at our college. Once they hit the main lobby upstairs, they're immediate blown away by the technology, the art and the wide open spaces in front of them. It's a visceral reaction and it's effective 99% of the time. Bankers and accountants are the rare exception - they immediately wonder how much all this amazing stuff cost – and they have no imagination to boot.

2. The Ultimate Audience(s)

While it's clear that you're building your workplace primarily for your employees, it's critical to remind yourself and your people that virtually every visitor to the space is a crucial part of your audience for one reason or another. And I really do mean almost "every" one.

I'm not talking simply about clients, customers, vendors, media, parents, students, business partners, regulators and other employers, I talking about everyone who comes to visit. We once saved a deal and closed on the last day of the month because our FedEx guy returned (basically on his own) to make a second re-delivery at our offices.

When we asked him why he would go out of his way at the end of his day to do that, he said he knew how seriously our receptionist took her job; he knew how important what we were waiting for was to us; and he wanted to do his part because he loved coming to our offices. He said it was one of the few places he visited where you could feel the energy and enthusiasm when you got off the elevator and you could just tell that everyone just cared. Culture is contagious and it starts at the front door.

3. The Main Message – 3 Key Themes

As you start to think about the environment, the impressions, and the culture that you're trying to create in your space, you need to appreciate that you're going to have to make some tough choices and pick a fairly narrow and focused message which you want to communicate clearly and <u>consistently</u> throughout the entire facility. You can't make everyone happy and you can't be all things to all people so you need to decide on what's most important to you and to the business and take your best shot. The worst possible strategy is always the straddle. Trying to address too many constituencies or too serve too many masters ends up with a messy, muddled and misplaced message. Go with what makes you proud and what you feel is the way to put your best foot forward. At least you'll know that one person is happy with the result.

The theme of your message will depend on the nature of your business and the phase of its development as well as a number of other factors. There are obviously many different themes, but 3 of them are commonly used in instances of start-ups or turnarounds where – if you do it right – you have a decent shot at starting with a relatively clean slate and inventing or re-inventing the vision as you go. The big 3 are these:

(a) Functionality – Transformation and Change

(b) Authenticity – All about Work and Accountability

(c) Aspiration – Creative Expression, Execution and Craft

Each of our last 3 projects presented a different challenge.

(a) *Kendall College* was a 75-year old failing college in desperate need of a turnaround and a transformation. Everything about the rebuilding of Kendall had to do with creating a flawless and technically advanced platform for the faculty of chefs to teach their culinary magic to successive generations of passionate students in a unique learning environment. Everything in the brand-new facility spoke to precision, professionalism and minute attention to detail and those messages formed the heart of the reborn culture of performance and excellence.

(b) *Experiencia's* two "worlds" – Exchange City (a collection of operating business in a 20,000 square foot "city") and Earthworks (4 distinct "natural" environments filled with real animals) – were practical work and learning environments for inner-city 4th and 5th graders, but they couldn't succeed as plastic or pretend places or as Disney-like fantasies. They needed to be grounded and serious places where the visiting students would achieve new levels of authentic responsibility, performance accountability, and team-based, peer-driven learning that they had never experienced before. Watching the students rise to the occasion and seize the new opportunities before them was an unforgettable daily experience.

(c) And finally, *Tribeca Flashpoint Academy's* message to a population of under-appreciated and under-served students – surrounded and encouraged by their true peers for the first time

in their lives – and challenged by the newest facilities, technologies and industry tools available – was very clear. The sky alone was the limit and everything was within their grasp if they made the commitment, had the passion, and did the work. It was all about craft, execution and aspirations – not to say dreams – and it became a special home for creative expression, collaborative and immersive learning, and the next generation of digital leaders for our country.

And when all the dust settles and all the paint dries and you finally get a chance to catch your breath and see what you've built - what you'll realize at the end of the journey is that it's in the building process itself – with all the messy twists and turns, upsets and mistakes – and all the pains and joys – all the highs and lows – that your team ultimately comes together and the fundamental foundation of your culture is formed.

It turns out that what you built is nowhere near as important as how you and your team went about the process of getting it built. Cultures are funny that way. You can try to explain it to people, but you can't understand it for them – they've got to live it to make it real.

TRICKED TRAFFIC ISN'T WORTH THE TROUBLE

An age-old question. If a tree falls in the forest, but there's no one there to hear it, does it make a sound? Who knows and who really cares? The better and more pressing question these days is: if the primary drivers for traffic to a website that you're paying money to advertise on are hacks, tricks and clever pet pix; what are the visitors who do show up (even assuming they are people and not tracking robots) really worth to you or anybody else?

I'd argue that they're not worth your time and certainly not worth any money you're paying for the very modest privilege of "entertaining" (in the loosest sense of the word) a bunch of morons with nothing better to do than to waste their time randomly clicking on just about anything. Instead of attracting people who might actually be interested in your products or services and also highly influential, you can end up spending money to attract mobs of easily-influenced people instead who probably couldn't explain how they go to the website if they were asked.

One of the things I always told restaurant owners about *Groupon* daily deals was that they were designed to attract "cheapies" to restaurants that were only looking for one-time deals instead of "foodies" who could become regular patrons and the true lifeblood of the business. And since I'm from Chicago and everyone's picking on *Groupon* these days, let me just say that we use it and that it makes sense for a lot of different kinds of businesses and situations IF you keep in mind 4 basic rules about when to do a daily-deals kind of deal:

1. The deal needs to drive new users and incremental revenue – not replace or cannibalize existing full margin revenues;

2. Your business can't be subject to capacity or size constraints which might result in the incremental traffic precluding access by and for existing customers and users;

3. The deal can't require you to spend or invest a great deal of upfront money with essentially sunk costs if the deal doesn't go; and

4. You can't put yourself in a position where taking on and delivering the deal gives you cash flow or other float problems.

But *Groupon* deals aside, there are still way too many companies "buying" into tonnage and volume (quantity rather than quality) and measuring their results by the wrong competitive metrics like "likes" and followers. As a result, the market continues to encourage young entrepreneurs to create (or basically make up) businesses which are all about buzz and bullshit rather than trying to build sustainable businesses which deliver real services and demonstrable results to clients and which have concrete economic rewards for those companies rather than cosmetic and superficial results that do nothing for any business's bottom line.

I keep seeing and hearing pitches and presentations predicated on prevarications, phony postings, and a pile of pictures that may be inexplicably popular, but have nothing really to do with anything and clearly nothing whatsoever to do with your products, services or business. As an example, I just sat through a highly-energized, but essentially empty, "presentation" about content and engagement which sadly, instead of being about ideas and approaches of substance, was all about scams and slick, but sleazy ploys to trick people into being traffic to sites for no good reason. A load of tactics and no real strategy or smarts. Or maybe they were really being just a little too smart for their own ultimate good. Because even if you're the biggest and fastest rat in the race, when the dust settles, you're still pretty much a rat.

STICK TO YOUR KNITTING

It turns out that the Three Musketeers had it half right. "All for one and one for all!" is a great strategy for assuring collaboration, teamwork and loyalty, but it can be a very dangerous approach in a start-up. This is because – notwithstanding the absolute best of intentions – it can lead to chaos in the kitchen with too many cooks and a whole lot of people trying to pitch in and "help out" who just end up being much more of a hindrance and a problem than if they simply minded their own business.

The fact is that, even if your business is short-handed and resource-constrained, you're not going to be well-served by people piling on to assist in areas where they don't have the skills, background or judgment to add value. Instead, they just get in the way or make things worse. Good intentions don't ever guarantee great results and, as the boss, you've got to politely tell these eager beavers to butt out. And you need to figure out a way to say "no thanks" without having them feel unappreciated, ignored or dismissed.

You don't want to crush their creativity or extinguish their enthusiasm, but you can't have your finance guys writing marketing copy (even in his alleged spare time) or your IT people trying to design your next product or service (unless perhaps you're in the IT business). And even then, if you are in the IT business, you still want your IT people taking care of their business and making sure that your servers and cloud connections don't blow up rather than suggesting new passionate, but sophisticated color schemes for your website.

Some skills are readily transferable and applicable across multiple disciplines, but too many people confuse energy, interest and even some skill with actual talent. I always loved it when I was making movies and people would dismiss a certain actor or actress and say that anyone could play that role. The truth is that the people up on the big screen are there for a reason – they have a certain electricity, attraction or whatever magic it is - and all the trying, practice, aspiration and desire won't ever help a million other wanna-bes duplicate their special presence. Stars are stars for a reason. They know that they can do one thing better than anyone else and the smartest ones do exactly that one thing and nothing else.

There's a reason that the people and companies that succeed in any line of business are those that focus their energy and resources and stick to their knitting. You need to be sure that both your company and your people have the same discipline. It's not even about what you actually say "yes" to and do, it's all about the many things that you have the guts to say "no" to and pass by even though they are terribly tempting.

This is all part of the process of what I'd call "getting real". It starts by admitting that democracy is not necessarily a virtue in all meetings; that not every idea is a good one or worth spending the group's time on; and that not everyone in the business is good at every part of the business or should be expected to be. And by the way, don't confuse bad ideas with bad intentions and don't forget that people can be terribly sincere and still have really stupid ideas.

It seems obvious, but I guarantee you that you'll find yourself stuck in these kinds of ultimately unproductive situations – especially as everyone in your company gets busier and busier – and the business continues to grow and expand. The basic nature of any start-up is a "let's get it done" attitude and, when things take longer than they should (with or without good reasons which may not be clear to everyone), there's a clear bias toward action – sometimes any action – and that's bad for everyone and really bad for the business because it encourages people who don't know what they're doing to roll up their sleeves and give themselves permission to try to do "something". Just because you can do something doesn't mean you should.

This is one of those cases where doing something really isn't necessarily better than doing nothing and waiting until the right people can get around to doing the thing that needs to get done and doing it the right way. It's hard for any entrepreneur to tell his people to hurry up and wait at the same time, but that's the right message. Stick to your knitting and mind your own part of the business.

SITUATIONAL ETHICS SUCKS

I'm afraid that we're developing another generation gap and this one isn't merely cosmetic (can't stand those tattoos!) or aurally aesthetic (can't stand that music!) or even extreme economic (why "own" anything). It's far more important than any of these fairly superficial differences and preferences – albeit I recognize that they are crushingly important to the hosts of *TMZ* and *Access Hollywood.*

And it's far more pressing and critical than the angst and quasi-parental concerns these weird choices engender in us grown-ups. I can deal with all the questionable choices that many young people are making today because I'm relatively sure that we all made similar (or much worse, but probably less long-lasting) choices in our youth and yet, amazingly enough, we're still here, standing tall, and giving them advice and the "benefit" of our wisdom – such as it is.

But I'm not talking about something that's a preference or an option that we can take or leave – I'm talking about a problem that threatens to undermine something so fundamental and basic to the conduct of business (and especially to early-stage angel investing) that almost everyone (other than those in the film or music business) has always taken it for gospel and for granted. They say every day in the film business, "I'll love you 'til I don't" so get used to it. But that kind of fleeting attachment or commitment and the complete absence of sincerity that's "just business" in those worlds isn't the way we hope and expect that the rest of the sane (and square) business world conducts itself.

That's why I'm getting increasingly concerned about this very basic idea. I recently heard Alan Matthew (a long-time successful options and commodities trader) express it forcefully in about 15 different ways throughout a recent talk he gave to several hundred entrepreneurs at 1871. He said that, in every deal he does, and in every transaction: "My word is my bond." And it's just that simple – especially in the trading pits in Chicago – where the entire ecosystem depends on trust and the ability for everyone to rely on the commitments and honesty of the other players. But the problem is that - even as essential a part as this attitude is to how we do business in Chicago - I don't think we're doing a good job of communicating this very critical concept to today's young entrepreneurs. Too many of them live in a different conceptual world – one driven by situational ethics. And it sucks.

Telling people half the story or what they want to hear instead of what they need to hear isn't a funding solution – it's an invitation to a later slaughter. And it's usually the entrepreneur and the management team who will ultimately get killed. So it makes sense to share ALL of the news all the time – if for no other reason than to just save yourself all the grief coming down the line. The truth never hurts unless it ought to and sometimes it's a powerful wake-up call for all concerned. There's never a really good or special time to decide to tell the truth – the time is all the time.

But, if you haven't been there (to make the right choice regardless of how hard or discouraging it may be or how it may impact your financing or prospects) and there's no one more experienced around to guide you because you're running full-speed ahead and you're also making it up as you go, it's far too easy to take a quick slide down that slippery ethical slope. And once you lose someone's confidence, once they come to believe that you don't share and abide by their fundamental values, you will never get their trust and support entirely back.

And, honestly, because a whole generation of kids have been told (at least since second grade) that they're amazing, exceptional and completely unique, it's just a short step for them to conclude that the ordinary rules don't apply to them and that morals are just for little people and that they're way above that somewhat mundane conformity and far too smart for it as well. An old friend of mine used to say – by way of excusing virtually anything disgusting that he managed to do - that exceptional people deserve special concessions. I'm afraid his disease may be spreading.

As I often <u>kiddingly</u> say when I'm talking about building your company's culture and instilling critical values in your people and your business processes: "These are my principles. If you don't like them, I have others." But that's always intended as a joke because – in the real world – we don't get to pick and choose when to honor our promises and commitments. We say what we'll do and then we do what we said we'd do. It couldn't be more straightforward – you don't get to be truthful some of the time or some time later or when it's a better or more convenient time. The truth doesn't vary based on circumstances.

And frankly, I'm not even sure that, in some cases, this is purely an issue of intentional dishonesty or immorality. I think it's just as much a lack of experience and education combined with way too much enthusiasm. Entrepreneurs can talk themselves into anything (I call this the "that hooker really liked me" condition) and, once they do, they want to sell it to the world. But whenever you find that you're having to shade the truth or forget some ugly facts in order to convince yourself or talk your team or some investor into something that you're not even sure you yourself buy off on, you're probably not doing yourself or anyone else a favor. It's almost inevitably a bad deal which you should back away from as quickly as possible.

And, while it's great to be highly motivated, it's not even a little cool if no one trusts your motives. It takes a time and hard work to build any kind of relationship, but just an instant and a suspicion (a long way from proof) to destroy it. And I know just how hard it is to say things that no one wants to hear, but that's part of the leader's job – it's not delegable and it's not optional.

It takes a great deal of experience and a whole bunch of broken dreams and busted relationships to appreciate that to be trusted is a much greater compliment than to be loved. Entrepreneurs – without a doubt – need and want (first and foremost) to be loved. It's part of the sickness which drives us. But, at the end of the day, trust is the only thing that you can really take to the bank.

WHY RABBITS DON'T RUN
BIG BUSINESSES

I've always been partial to Thumper's Dad's advice about communication. In case you don't recall it from the *Bambi* movie, his Dad said: "If you can't say something nice, don't say nothin' at all" - at least as Thumper recalled it. And, as it happens, this is pretty good advice for small talking animals, but it's a really bad way to run your company. You can't build a successful business based on a culture that values quiet, courtesy and consensus over honest conversations, constructive criticism and confrontations where necessary. Politely keeping the peace can't ever trump telling the truth. The best operators know two things for certain: (1) the truth only hurts when you don't tell it and (2) the truth only hurts when it should. I realize that sometimes it's very hard to tell the truth, but it's just as hard to hide it and a whole lot less productive.

White lies and other pleasantries are worthless – they're a lot like eating junk food – you get a temporary lift, but no nourishment; the problem persists; the emptiness returns; and nothing gets done in the meantime. And when you encourage people to lie even a little, you learn quickly that people who will lie for you will eventually lie to you. Better a few bruises and battered egos than a bankrupt business based on bullshitting each other. And honestly, it's just so much easier for everyone because when you always tell the truth, you never have to waste time and energy trying to remember your lies.

Frankly, an aggressive culture where people stand their ground and argue their cases makes for much better ultimate decisions as long as people are arguing for the right reasons. The right reasons are to get to the truth and the best results for the business and not because people need to be right and won't shut up until they grind everyone down and wear everyone else out. Make your point; say your piece; and sit your butt down. Don't argue with the truth.

You want your people to fearlessly face the facts. As one of the great old Hollywood moguls used to say: "I want my people to tell me the truth even if it costs them their jobs". But seriously, unpleasant facts don't fade away when you ignore them – they fester – and refusing to look at them won't change the situation or improve things until you do something about them. Facts may change, but the truth never does. And waiting only makes things worse. It's a funny thing about the truth – the truth doesn't have a time of its own. There's never a better or best time to tell someone the truth – the time for truth is always <u>now</u>.

I think all of the foregoing comes down to a few simple "rules" which you need to share (somewhat obsessively) with all of your people (not just newbies in orientations) on a regular and recurring basis. My suggested and very basic rules are as follows:

1. Tell the Truth

    No shades, no strokes, no "smoothing" the news or softening the blows – give it to me simple and straight. Figures don't lie, but they often don't tell the whole story. Make sure that the metrics don't get in the way of a clear message. As they say, everyone is entitled to their own opinion, but the facts are the facts – you don't get to pick and choose them.

2. Tell It Timely

    Nothing ugly really improves over time. Don't wait to bring me bad news. The sooner and shorter the better. I need a brief, not as book. Nothing elaborate – just accurate information delivered on time and in time.

3. Tell Everyone

    Don't assume that everyone else (or anyone else) necessarily knows what you know. Spread the word. In addition to the general virtues of transparency and making sure that eventually the message does get thru to the right people; going wide makes it more likely that meaningful and actionable information will also get to people who need whether you even realize that or not.

4. Tell It 'til Someone Listens

    I don't think that, in most businesses, you can ever over-communicate relevant and time-sensitive data. But you will often encounter people who fall into two problem piles: (a) people who don't want to say what nobody wants to hear; and (b) people who don't want to hear what needs to and has to be said and spread throughout the organization. These folks are master manipulators and they typically follow the standard three-step routine in dealing with "inconvenient", but sadly true facts: (i) first they aggressively ridicule; (ii) then they violently resist; and finally (iii) they get with the program – claim that they knew it all along – and treat things as obvious and self-evident. You need to keep spreading the word until you're sure that you've done as much as you can reasonably do to let the folks in charge know what you know. If they don't listen after that, so be it. It's frustrating and depressing, but in many businesses, it's a fact of life. As Bruce Springsteen says: "When the truth is spoken and it makes no difference – something in your heart goes cold". After a while, if it's clear that you're wasting your breath, find a better place to be.

5. Tell It All the Time

And finally, truth-telling is not a sometime thing. As with everything else that matters in your business, it's an everyday, all day part of creating and maintaining an environment where the organization learns and grows and where things continue to improve through a constant iterative process. You can't make innovation through iteration work if you don't have a constant and accurate flow of data telling you what's working and what's not and where you're going wrong.

WHAT I LEARNED FROM
MY WAITRESS

I believe in life-long learning. I also believe that you can learn something of value from almost anyone. Everyone's an example - sometimes a good example - sometimes not - but always instructive. The key is to extract the wisdom from the wood chips and apply the lessons to your own work and/or life. It's easier said than done. For years, I've had a favorite waitress at my neighborhood deli named Brenda. I hate to wait for anything, but I'm happy to wait for a seat in her section because I think she actually improves my digestion. And she always shows me something. This week I learned three important things. It's always somewhat remarkable because very few people actually get tips <u>from</u> their waitress. So pay attention.

  1. Repeat After Me.

I noticed that she has her own way of taking orders. She repeats everything that I say right back to me – word for word. And there's a curious comfort in that which is very reassuring. How many times have you had some smart-ass waiter stand there while you're reciting your very complicated choices and requirements and not write anything down or repeat a single thing? Did you really feel confident that your food was going to fill the bill or were you just a little anxious that maybe Wally the Waiter didn't really have the world's greatest memory and that your potatoes were coming with peppers whether you liked it or not? Not exactly the warm and fuzzy feeling that makes for return visits.

But the most important part of her process actually wasn't that she always got my order right. Her mimicry sent me a specific and powerful message. Not only was I being listened to; I was being heard. And I was being heard by someone who actually cared about me and about getting my order right. That emotional impression - that recurring result - the ineffable feeling of being "important" and cared for - is the absolute heart of great customer service. Getting the order right is basic execution. Getting the listening part of the process correct – basically adding communication to the conversation - was even more important. It's that old cliché – I don't really care how much you know until I know how much you care.

Way too often today we're distracted when we're supposed to be listening. We're texting or typing. We're multi-tasking or (not so discretely) checking our monitors for new email. And we're sending a very clear message to the person(s) talking to us. It says "I might seem to be listening, but you're not really being heard because my mind and my attention are obviously elsewhere" or it could be saying "I'm actually anywhere, but here in the moment and you don't really matter." Frankly, nothing could be worse for your people, your customers or your business.

If your customers don't think you're concerned about them or listening to them, they won't be customers for long. And it's even worse internally. If your people bring you problems or concerns and you seem too busy to listen or to be bothered, it won't take them too long to conclude that you don't care. They'll stop coming to you and, far more critically, they'll stop caring themselves. It's when your people stop bringing you their problems that you know you have a real problem.

So, if you're going to have a meeting - make it as short as possible - make sure it's necessary and not window dressing or make-work - and make sure it matters (so you aren't meeting for the sake of meeting). And then, if you're gonna do it - do it right. Be there 100%. Pay attention. Listen carefully. Take notes. Give them some feedback and a reaction. Make sure your people know they're being heard.

2. Do What You Can Do.

My waitress doesn't own her restaurant and therefore she doesn't get to set the prices on the menu or the size of the portions. She doesn't determine the daily specials and she can't guarantee that they've got my favorite fruit on any given morning. Sometimes there are things simply beyond her control – like a new cook or busboy who just can't get things right. And shame on her for forgetting the surcharge for sharing. And - heaven forbid - she better not ignore the "no substitutions" rule which apparently is the Eleventh Commandment of the Bible of the restaurant business. So, given the many things that can get in the way of her delivering the kind of service and experience which makes a difference to her customers, she has developed her own simple strategy. She does what she can.

That may sound simplistic and somewhat random, but it's not that at all. This isn't some arbitrary process. It isn't a case of flouting the fat cats or trying to get away with something. The fact is that it's good for business to take care of your "friends" - the regulars - the special customers who represent the recurring foundation of the business. And that's exactly what she does and here's how she does it.

You say you don't want the green beans that come with your meat loaf. But the rules say "No Substitutes". Well, she doesn't substitute anything – she just piles on extra potatoes and lets you know it's a double portion. Not so good for the waist line, but great for making sure you know you're special. She can't change the rules, but she works her magic with the ladle. She works with what she has control over and she does what she can and it shows and – believe me - it matters. This is her own individual solution. When you incorporate this kind of flexibility and empowerment into your entire organization, you become Nordstrom's – the epitome of empowered employees and a great place to shop.

The trick that can make a difference in your own business is to figure out how to encourage initiative and how to give all of your people permission to make things special for your customers in their own personal way.

3.   Don't Worry, Be Happy

If our jobs were fun every day, I think they'd eventually change the name and stop calling it "work". But at the end of the day, every job turns out to be a direct reflection of the amount of time, effort, commitment and passion you put into it. There are really no boring jobs; just people who are bored with their jobs because they lack the energy, attitude and imagination to make something great out of every day. The best bosses I know make it their business to find the pumped-up people in their places and make sure that their excitement, enthusiasm and energy is shared and communicated throughout the organization.

What I love about Brenda the waitress is that she absolutely refuses to let anyone be the "bad" in her day. On her worst day, she's a smile waiting to happen and you just can't knock her off her stride because she makes it her business to make your day in some little way. Her enthusiasm is absolutely authentic and completely contagious. There's no question that it's possible to take the joy out of any job. But you couldn't get her down if your life depended on it. This isn't just about being Peppy Pearl every day – it turns out to be communicating a different and far more important message.

It's about attitude and respect. It says that her job may not be rocket science or Earth-shatteringly important – but she takes great pride in how she does it and she puts herself entirely into the process. She expects you to appreciate that and to respect her effort and commitment to doing the best job of her job that she can do every day. And, unless you're completely unconscious, you do.

ABOUT THE AUTHOR

Howard Tullman is the CEO of 1871 in Chicago where digital startups get their start.

He is also the General Managing Partner of two venture funds: Chicago High-Tech Investment Partners and G2T3V, LLC which focuses on funding disruptiveinnovators. He is the former Chairman and CEO of Tribeca Flashpoint Media Arts Academy in Chicago.

He is an active member of numerous city, state and civic boards and organizations and a tireless supporter and mentor to many start-ups and other businesses and individuals. He has successfully founded more than a dozen high-tech businesses in his 50 year career and created more than $1 billion in investor value as well as thousands of new jobs.

He writes a regular weekly blog on The Perspiration Principles for Inc. Magazine and can be directly contacted by email at h@g2t3v.com or *h@1871.com* or at tullman@ aol.com, tullman@chicago.com, @tullman, or *thru his blog:tullman.blogspot.com* or his primary website: *www. tullman.com.*

You can read all of Howard's Perspiration Principles in one download by visiting *http://BlogIntoBook.com/tullman/.*